Dear Parents and Educators,

Welcome to Penguin Young Readers! As parents and educators, you know that each child develops at his or her own pace—in terms of speech, critical thinking, and, of course, reading. Penguin Young Readers recognizes this fact. As a result, each Penguin Young Readers book is assigned a traditional easy-to-read level (1–4) as well as a Guided Reading Level (A–P). Both of these systems will help you choose the right book for your child. Please refer to the back of each book for specific leveling information. Penguin Young Readers features esteemed authors and illustrators, stories about favorite characters, fascinating nonfiction, and more!

Watch Out!
The World's Most Dangerous Creatures

LEVEL 3

GUIDED READING LEVEL **M**

This book is perfect for a **Transitional Reader** who:
- can read multisyllable and compound words;
- can read words with prefixes and suffixes;
- is able to identify story elements (beginning, middle, end, plot, setting, characters, problem, solution); and
- can understand different points of view.

Here are some **activities** you can do during and after reading this book:
- Vocabulary: Find the words below in the text. Does the child know the definitions? Can the child use picture or text clues to figure out the meanings? If not, use a dictionary to look up the words.

amphibians	larvae	prey	tentacles
frenzy	predator	stalk	venom

- Comprehension: After reading the book, answer the following questions:
  - What is the heaviest snake in the world?
  - How did the bullet ant get its name?
  - Where do black widow spiders live?

Remember, sharing the love of reading with a child is the best gift you can give!

—Bonnie Bader, EdM
   Penguin Young Readers program

*Penguin Young Readers are leveled by independent reviewers applying the standards developed by Irene Fountas and Gay Su Pinnell in *Matching Books to Readers: Using Leveled Books in Guided Reading*, Heinemann, 1999.

In memory of Steve Irwin,
the Crocodile Hunter, whose passion for
finding the beauty in dangerous creatures
still inspires me—GLC

To Bev & Alex Gair: Because you enjoy these
books as much as the youngsters do—PM

Penguin Young Readers
Published by the Penguin Group
Penguin Group (USA) Inc., 375 Hudson Street, New York, New York 10014, USA
Penguin Group (Canada), 90 Eglinton Avenue East, Suite 700, Toronto, Ontario M4P 2Y3, Canada
(a division of Pearson Penguin Canada Inc.)
Penguin Books Ltd., 80 Strand, London WC2R 0RL, England
Penguin Group Ireland, 25 St. Stephen's Green, Dublin 2, Ireland (a division of Penguin Books Ltd.)
Penguin Group (Australia), 250 Camberwell Road, Camberwell, Victoria 3124, Australia
(a division of Pearson Australia Group Pty. Ltd.)
Penguin Books India Pvt. Ltd., 11 Community Centre, Panchsheel Park, New Delhi—110 017, India
Penguin Group (NZ), 67 Apollo Drive, Rosedale, Auckland 0632, New Zealand
(a division of Pearson New Zealand Ltd.)
Penguin Books (South Africa) (Pty.) Ltd., 24 Sturdee Avenue,
Rosebank, Johannesburg 2196, South Africa

Penguin Books Ltd., Registered Offices: 80 Strand, London WC2R 0RL, England

Library of Congress Control Number: 2010028168

ISBN 978-0-448-45108-4   10 9 8

PENGUIN YOUNG READERS

LEVEL
3
TRANSITIONAL
READER

WATCH OUT!
THE WORLD'S MOST DANGEROUS CREATURES

by Ginjer L. Clarke
illustrated by Pete Mueller

Penguin Young Readers
An Imprint of Penguin Group (USA) Inc.

Introduction

Where are dangerous animals found? Everywhere! Some are even hidden in our backyards. You would never know that danger was lurking nearby. These creatures use teeth, tentacles, fangs, claws, and spines to kill animals and sometimes people.

The colorful lionfish blends into the coral on the seabed. The stonefish looks like a rock at the bottom of the ocean. But do not be fooled! These fish have venomous spines that can hurt and sometimes kill.

What other animals are dangerous? Let's read and find out!

Chapter 1
Scary Sea Creatures

The **tiger shark** gets its name from the dark stripes on its back that look like a tiger's stripes. It eats almost anything that it can swallow, including fish, squid, sea turtles, seals, and small sharks. It sometimes eats weird things like license plates and paint cans that fall to the bottom of the ocean!

This tiger shark swims into warm, shallow water at night. It waits just below the water for a seabird to land. *Snap!* It quickly grabs the bird. Its terrible teeth rip and tear through the bird's bones. The shark swims off to rest after its feeding frenzy.

The **great barracuda** is a fierce
fish. It grows up to six feet long.
Its teeth are as sharp as knives.
The barracuda's long body helps
it swim superfast to catch prey.
The barracuda is very curious and
will chase anything that splashes,
including divers and swimmers.

This barracuda stays still near a deep ocean reef. Its big eyes can see well, even in cloudy, dark water. A smaller fish swims by. The barracuda takes off. *Chomp!* The barracuda grabs the fish in its powerful jaws. The fish does not stand a chance!

The **blue-ringed octopus** is only eight inches long, but it is deadly. It is usually orange-brown, but bright blue rings appear on its body when it feels threatened. The blue rings warn animals to keep away from this octopus.

Sometimes people pick up a blue-ringed octopus to look at it. They do not know it is dangerous. *Nip!* The octopus bites gently, but its venom works fast. The person stops breathing and can die within hours if he or she is not treated in a hospital. This little octopus is big trouble!

Some stingrays have blue spots,
too. The **blue-spotted stingray**
lies buried in the ocean floor, with
only its eyes sticking out. Swimmers
sometimes step on stingrays because
they are hidden in the sand.
Stingrays do not attack people,
but they fight back when they get
stepped on.

Whap! A blue-spotted stingray whips its tail and cuts the swimmer with its blue, swordlike spine. The spine is so sharp that it can cut through wet suits and shoes. Stingray venom is very painful, but people do not usually die from it. Remember to shuffle your feet when you walk in the ocean so you don't step on a stingray!

The **box jellyfish** is the most dangerous creature in the water. These jellyfish have killed more people than stonefish, sharks, and crocodiles combined. The box jellyfish looks like a bell-shaped blob with up to 60 tentacles hanging down. It is hard to see in the water.

This box jellyfish waits for prey to bump into its tentacles. *Zap!* It stings a small shrimp and eats it quickly.

Swimmers in the waters off Australia have died in just a few minutes after touching a box jellyfish. Scientists are not sure how, but sea turtles can eat them without being stung!

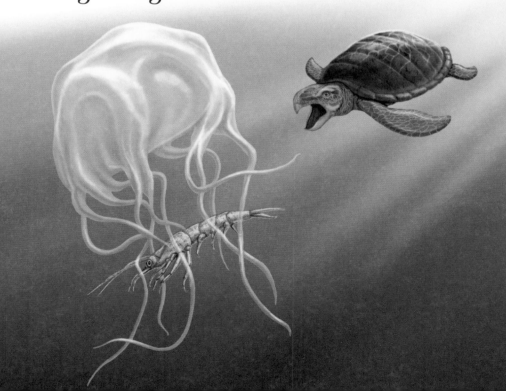

Chapter 2
Reptiles and Amphibians

Even other venomous snakes fear the deadly **king cobra**. It is the largest venomous snake and can grow up to 18 feet long. It lives mostly in Asia. The king cobra does not have the strongest venom, but its bite contains a lot of venom. Just one cobra bite has enough venom to kill an elephant.

Female cobras are most dangerous when defending their nests. *Hiss!* This king cobra rears up and spreads her hood to look bigger. The cobra warns another snake to keep away from her eggs. The other snake does not back off, so the cobra strikes and bites it. The cobra swallows the snake while it is still alive.

The **green anaconda** is the heaviest snake in the world. It can weigh up to 500 pounds. The anaconda does not attack people. It eats large prey like deer, boars, jaguars, and caimans. The anaconda kills large animals by constricting, or squeezing, them until they cannot breathe.

This anaconda glides through the Amazon River in South America. It can stay underwater for up to 10 minutes waiting for its prey. A boar comes to the river to drink. *Whoosh!* The anaconda pops up. It bites the boar quickly and drags it into the river. The snake constricts the boar and then eats it whole.

The **Nile crocodile** can grow up to 20 feet long and can weigh more than 1,500 pounds—as much as three anacondas! The Nile crocodile can move quickly to catch animals at the water hole. It attacks zebras, antelopes, lions, warthogs, buffalo, and people.

This crocodile hides in a river.
Boom! It leaps at a zebra. The
crocodile clamps onto the zebra and
takes it down. The crocodile does a
"death roll" around and around in
circles. The zebra drowns, and the
croc slowly eats the whole thing.

The **Komodo dragon** is the world's largest lizard. It lives on Komodo Island and several other islands in Indonesia. The Komodo dragon runs fast. It can catch and kill pigs, deer, monkeys, other Komodo dragons, and sometimes even people.

It cannot hear or see well, but it can smell food from miles away.

This Komodo dragon smells the air with its long, forked tongue. A goat wanders nearby, and the Komodo dragon chases it. *Rip!* The Komodo dragon catches the goat and pulls it to pieces. What a messy eater!

Poison dart frogs are among the most poisonous animals. Poison from the frogs' skin has been used on the tips of darts to kill animals and people. These little frogs can be blue, red, yellow, or green, and they all have black spots. The bright colors of these frogs warn the other animals of the rain forest to keep away.

A snake tries to grab a blue dart frog and gets a nasty surprise. Poison on the frog's skin hurts the snake when it licks the frog. *Ouch!* The frog's poison is deadly if the snake swallows the frog. The snake moves on to find a tastier meal.

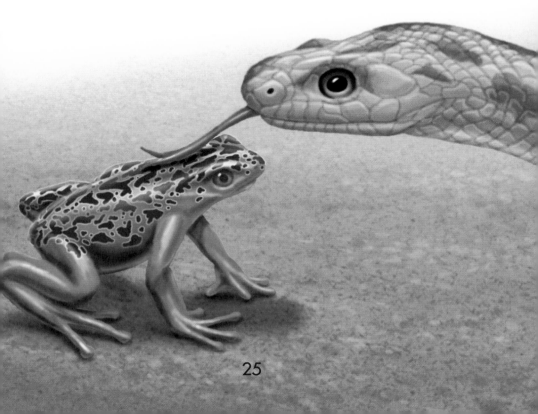

Chapter 3
Deadly Mammals

Elephants are usually peaceful. But male **African elephants** use their long, sharp tusks to fight over who is in charge. Male elephants can be very aggressive and dangerous. They sometimes attack people and destroy crops and forests.

Crash! These two male elephants lock their trunks and push. They are fighting over a female. They use their tusks like swords to hit and stab each other until one of them gives up. What a battle of beasts!

The word **hippopotamus** comes
from the Greek word for "river horse."
Hippos may look lazy as they float in
the rivers of Africa, but they can move
quickly when they want to. Hippos will
kill animals or people when they feel
threatened. They have attacked boats
and trampled people on land.

Roar! This hippo warns a crocodile to keep away from her baby. She opens her jaws wide to show her enormous bottom teeth. The crocodile does not back off. The hippo charges and bites the croc. That shows the crocodile that the hippo is the boss around here!

Polar bear babies are cute, but the adults are dangerous. They fight one another and kill walruses and sometimes people. But they mostly eat seals. Polar bears either stalk seals or sit very still and wait for them to come out of the water.

This polar bear is sitting quietly by a hole in the Arctic ice. Suddenly, a seal pops up for air. *Smash!* The polar bear grabs the seal with his huge paw. He bites the seal on the head, and the seal dies instantly. Polar bears need a lot of food to stay warm in the winter.

The **Bengal tiger** is one of the world's most feared predators. Healthy, well-fed tigers in other places do not usually hurt people. But about 250 Bengal tigers live in a part of India called the Sunderbans (say: SOON-der-bon). These Bengal tigers eat mostly deer, but they are also man-eaters. No one knows exactly why.

This tiger crouches in the grass. It is quietly watching a buffalo drink at the water hole at night. *Pounce!* The tiger jumps on the buffalo from behind. It bites the buffalo in the throat with its long, top teeth. The buffalo falls down dead.

Did you know rats can be deadly? Rats live everywhere people live. **Brown rats** are the most common. These rats spread diseases like rabies. The fleas that live on the rats bite people and can make them sick. Millions of people have died from the diseases carried by rats.

Brown rats will eat anything. They often go into grocery stores and restaurants to look for food. These places have to be kept clean to keep the food safe and the rats away. Brown rats travel in packs of up to 200. They swarm in garbage dumps, sewers, and underground burrows. These nasty animals are everywhere!

Chapter 4
Arachnids and Insects

Scorpions are scary-looking! All 1,500 species of scorpions have venom in their stingers, but only about 25 types can actually kill people. Thousands of people die every year from scorpion stings, mostly in Mexico, North Africa, and the Middle East.

The **deathstalker** is small, but it is one of the deadliest scorpions. Its venom is strong and painful.

This deathstalker prowls the desert. It spots a praying mantis. *Pow!* The deathstalker arches its stinger and jabs the mantis. It breaks the mantis into pieces with its pincers and eats it up.

Most spiders are not dangerous, but some have bites that can kill. The **black widow** is one of the deadliest spiders in the world. It lives in warm places everywhere. Only female black widows are deadly.

This black widow spins a cobweb made of tangled silk threads. It

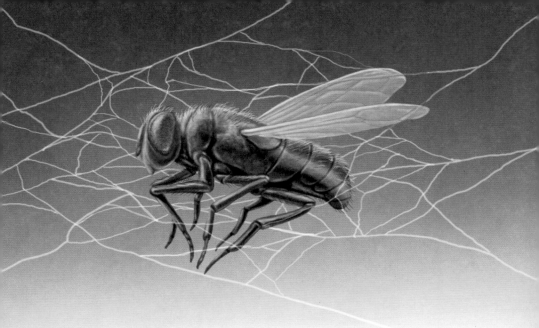

has a red mark on its belly that
looks like two triangles touching.
She catches flies, moths, ants, and
other spiders in her web. *Gotcha!* A
fly lands on the web, and the spider
wraps it in sticky silk. The spider
shoots venom into the fly that turns
its insides into liquid. Then the
spider sucks out the fly's guts.

The **Asian giant hornet** is the largest hornet in the world. This hornet lives mostly in Japan. It is almost as big as your hand, with a wingspan of three inches. The giant hornet has a big stinger filled with deadly venom. The venom is so strong that it can melt human flesh!

Zoom! These giant hornets attack a honeybee hive. The hornets use their mouthparts to bite off the honeybees' heads. In only a couple of hours, a few hornets can kill all the bees. The hornets steal the bees' larvae and feed them to their own larvae. What horrible hornets!

The **bullet ant** has the most painful bite of any insect. It is called a bullet ant because its bite feels as painful as being shot by a bullet from a gun. The pain is described as a burning and throbbing sensation that lasts for a day.

Bullet ants can grow to be up to one inch long with big pincers. They live in the rain forests of Central and South America.

Bullet ants sting to attack prey and to defend their nests.

These ants swarm out of their nest when flies start attacking it. *Shriek!* The ants warn the flies by making sounds with their bodies. Then the ants bite the flies. The flies die from the venom. These are big, bad bullet ants!

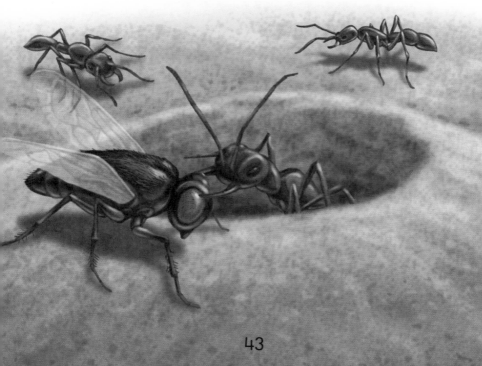

What creature kills the most people? The tiny **mosquito**. Mosquitoes carry many diseases, like malaria and yellow fever. These diseases kill millions of people all over the world every year. Only female mosquitoes suck blood. They need the energy to lay their eggs. Male mosquitoes drink plant juices, and they are harmless.

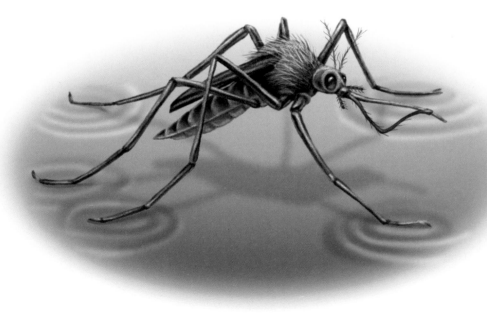

The female mosquito lays her eggs in standing water, like puddles. The mosquito finds a target by sensing body heat and smell. *Buzz!*

This female mosquito lands on a person's arm and pokes in her sharp mouthpart. She fills up her body with blood. What a pesky little creature!

There is another dangerous creature that is even smaller than a mosquito. **Helminths** are little worms that live inside people's bodies. Different kinds of helminths are flukes, roundworms, and tapeworms. They get inside us when we eat food with their eggs inside or when we are bitten by insects that have them.

Helminths grow bigger by eating the food in your intestines. This can cause cramps and pain. Helminths can grow to be up to 30 feet long. People have to take medicine to get rid of these nasty worms, or they can die from infection. Most people who get these worms live in warm, tropical places.

Most dangerous animals try to stay away from people because we sometimes hurt them, too. Keep away from them, and they will probably leave you alone. But beware and watch out . . . these creatures can be deadly!

SCHOLASTIC
News
Nonfiction Readers®

Our Earth
Saving Energy

by Peggy Hock

Children's Press®
An Imprint of Scholastic Inc.
New York Toronto London Auckland Sydney
Mexico City New Delhi Hong Kong
Danbury, Connecticut

These content vocabulary word builders are for grades 1–2.

Content Adviser: Zoe Chafe, Research Associate, Worldwatch Institute, Washington, DC

Reading Consultant: Cecilia Minden-Cupp, PhD, Early Literacy Consultant and Author, Chapel Hill, North Carolina

Photographs © 2009: age fotostock: 5 top right, 6 (Adam Crowley), 5 bottom right (Photodisc); Alamy Images: 17 (Angela Hampton Picture Library), 23 bottom left (Imagebroker), 21 top (JupiterImages/Brand X), 4 bottom left, 8 left (Paul Kuroda), 23 top left (Mediacolors), 7 (Ian Shaw), 5 top left, 9 inset (Paul Thompson Images); Corbis Images: 4 top, 11 (Jon Hicks), 23 bottom right (Frithjof Hirdes/zefa), bottom left, 9 main (Larry Lee Photography); Digital Light Source/Hutchings Stock Photography: back cover, 20 bottom; Getty Images: 23 top right (Panoramic Images), 20 top left (Julie Toy); iStockphoto/Denis Vorob'yev: 15 left; Masterfile: 2, 15 right, 20 top right, 21 center left (Robert George Young), 13, 19; Monty Stilson: cover; Photo Researchers, NY/Astrid & Hanns-Frieder Michler: 4 bottom right, right; PhotoEdit/David Young-Wolff: 21 center right; VEER/Brand X Photography: 21 bottom.

Book Design: Simonsays Design!
Book Production: The Design Lab

Library of Congress Cataloging-in-Publication Data
Hock, Peggy, 1948–
Saving energy / By Peggy Hock.
    p. cm.—(Scholastic news nonfiction readers)
Includes bibliographical references and index.
ISBN-13: 978-0-531-13835-9 (lib. bdg.) 978-0-531-20435-1 (pbk.)
ISBN-10: 0-531-13835-6 (lib. bdg.) 0-531-20435-9 (pbk.)
1. Energy conservation—Juvenile literature. I. Title. II. Series.
TJ163.35.H63 2008
333.79—dc22
                                           2007051898

CONTENTS

WORD HUNT

Look for these words as you read. They will be in **bold**.

air pollution
(ayr puh-**loo**-shuhr

gasoline
(gas-uh-**leen**)

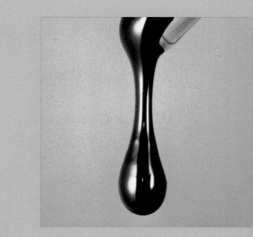

oil
(oyl)

4

coal
(kohl)

electrical outlet
(ih-**lek**-trih-kuhl
out-let)

power plant
(**pow**-uhr plant)

recycle
(ree-**sye**-kuhl)

Using Energy

Look around. Can you see where energy is being used?

Energy is used to heat buildings and run cars.

Energy is also used by everything that plugs into an **electrical outlet**.

electrical outlet

How many different ways do you use energy each day?

People use **oil** and **coal** to get much of the energy they need.

Oil is used to make **gasoline** for cars.

Coal and natural gas are burned in **power plants**.

gasoline

oil

coal

Many power plants burn coal to make electricity.

Burning coal, oil, and other things creates **air pollution**.

That is one reason to use less energy.

Someday, people may not be able to find enough oil and coal to use.

That is another good reason to save energy!

What can you do to save energy?

Big cities like Los Angeles have air pollution. Air pollution is not healthy for people.

Saving gas is one way to save energy.

Taking fewer car trips saves gas.

Could you ride your bike or walk to school?

That would save gas.

Taking the bus saves gas, too.

A bus can hold many kids. Getting all these kids to school in cars would use a lot more gas.

How else can you save energy?

You can save energy by using less electricity.

Turn off the lights when you leave a room.

Make sure to turn off computers and TVs when you are not using them.

The funny-looking lightbulb on the right helps people save energy. It uses much less energy than the regular lightbulb.

Another way to save energy is to use less plastic.

Making plastic and other things in factories uses a lot of energy.

Use plastic packages more than once, if you can.

And remember to **recycle**. It takes less energy to make things from recycled plastic than from new plastic.

Recycling plastic, paper, and metal helps save energy.

17

Can you think of other ways to save energy at school and at home?

Talk to an adult and share your ideas.

Then make your own energy-saving plan!

You can save energy by turning off the TV when you are done watching it.

Five Easy Ways to Save Energy

1 ·········

Put on a
sweater
instead of
turning up
the heat in
winter.

2 ·····················

Cut down on car trips.
Bike, carpool, or take a
bus when you can.

5

Open a window and use a fan instead of an air conditioner in the summer.

4

Recycle and buy recycled products.

3

Turn off the lights when you leave a room.

21

YOUR NEW WORDS

air pollution (ayr puh-**loo**-shuhn) harmful materials that make the air dirty and unhealthy to breathe

coal (kohl) a hard, black rock that is burned to produce electricity

electrical outlet (ih-**lek**-trih-kuhl **out**-let) an opening in a wall that leads to a source of electricity

gasoline (gas-uh-**leen**) liquid fuel that is made from oil found underground

oil (oyl) a thick liquid found underground that is used to make gasoline and other products

power plants (**pow**-uhr plants) places where fuel is burned to make electricity

recycle (ree-**sye**-kuhl) to make old plastic, paper, glass, and metal into new objects

WHERE CAN ENERGY COME FROM?

Coal or oil (or natural gas, not shown)

Moving water

Sunshine

Wind

INDEX

FIND OUT MORE

Book:
Green, Jen. *Why Should I Save Energy?* Hauppauge, NY: Barron's Educational Series, Inc., 2005.

Website:
Energy Quest
http://www.energyquest.ca.gov

MEET THE AUTHOR

Peggy Hock lives near San Francisco, California. She likes to go backpacking with her husband and two grown children. She uses compact fluorescent lightbulbs in her lamps.